MW01170800

DATING 101

ben young and
dr. samuel adams

NELSON BOOKS
A Division of Thomas Nelson Publishers
Since 1798

www.thomasnelson.com

Published in Nashville, Tennessee, by Thomas Nelson, Inc.

Nelson Books titles may be purchased in bulk for educational, business, fund-raising, or sales promotional use. For information, please e-mail SpecialMarkets@ThomasNelson.com.

Scripture quotations are from the HOLY BIBLE: NEW INTERNATIONAL VERSION®. Copyright © 1973, 1978, 1984 by International Bible Society. Used by permission of Zondervan Publishing House. All rights reserved.

Names and stories in this book are based on actual incidents. However, all names and details have been changed to protect privacy.

Library of Congress Cataloging-in-Publication Data

Dating 101 / Ben Young and Samuel Adams.
    p. cm.
    ISBN 0-7852-8794-9 (hardcover)
    1. Dating (Social customs) 2. Dating (Social customs)—Religious aspects—Christianity. 3. Mate selection—Religious aspects—Christianity. 4. Christian youth—Conduct of life.
I. Adams, Sam (Samuel) II. Title. III. Title: Dating one-o-one.
IV. Title: Dating one hundred one. V. Title: Dating one hundred and one.
    HQ801.Y674 2006
    646.7'7—dc22
    2006019090

Printed in the United States of America

06 07 08 09 WOR 6 5 4 3 2 1

Contents

Introduction

Welcome to *Dating 101*. There are perhaps several reasons why you picked up this book. You may be tired of the dating scene, tired of pouring time, energy, and money into relationships that start off great and end with heartache. Maybe you are frustrated because you can't find The One for you, no matter how hard you pray, primp, and plead. Maybe you just came out of a serious relationship that bombed, and you can't figure out why. Or maybe the dating scene is new for you and you feel overwhelmed. You need a road map to guide you through the wonderful, yet ever-so-frightening land called *Dating*.

I (Ben) remember there were times in my dating career when I felt so confused and put out with the whole system, I thought my brain would explode. I began to write down quips and theories (like "The Platonic Relationship Theory," "The Heisman Trophy Treatment," and "The Heavy Metal Headbanger Trap"). After a few years, I coined nearly fifty dating terms, a collection we call "Swami Ben's Theories and Observations on the Mixed-Up, Crazy World of Relationships." Granted, I was no relationship swami, but through experience and a lot of thought, I was learning how to make the dating thing really work.

Finally, the dating thing worked in my life and not just in my theories. God did not answer my bogus prayer request to arrange a marriage or turn me into a monk, but He did allow me to meet the woman of my dreams, learn how to grow in this relationship, and eventually get married. Finding such a woman was well worth the years of pain, struggle, and loneliness.

During a decade of working with thousands of singles and gleaning wisdom from my own dating experiences, I began to discover not just relationship theories, but relationship laws that, if you kept them, you would be blessed, and if you broke them, you would be cursed. I called my good friend, clinical psychologist, Dr. Sam

Adams, to see if my observations were based in reality or if I was just delusional. He verified that I was not insane, and told me he also believed there were some absolutes in the dating process. We decided to combine my street-smart insights and observations of relationships with his clinical knowledge and counseling expertise, and this book, along with three others, is the result.

CORE CURRICULUM

In college, everybody has to take a few required courses called "core curriculum" in order to graduate. The courses don't go into great depth about the subject but provide you with enough information so that you can understand the basics. You may not be ready to give a lecture on the migratory habits of monarch butterflies after Biology 101, but you could at least tell someone why grass is green. Consider *Dating 101* as part of your core curriculum. We want to equip you with the basics of how to survive in the world of dating, so you steer clear of the pitfalls and greatly increase your odds of finding a successful relationship. We promise to stay away from contemporary, relativistic dating theories. Our goal is not to tickle your ears or fill your mind with pseudo-psychological platitudes on relationships. There is enough bad advice on dating being spewed out on TV sitcoms and talk shows to fill legions of singles bars and health clubs. This book will give you practical, no-nonsense do's and don'ts on how to make dating work (and please don't be offended by our political incorrectness). Keep in mind, these are not suggestions or recommendations based upon surveys and opinion polls. These are solid "truths" that, for the most part, have a moral foundation. *Dating 101* will introduce you to steps to make your relationships run more smoothly, so you can avoid the heartbreaking side of dating and be on your way to building a loving, lasting relationship.

In a society that says there are no absolute truths—all truth is relative—some of our dating advice may sound a bit old-fashioned at times. But we believe that the Bible has some absolute truths that can guide us, either directly or indirectly, toward building successful relationships. Every relationship will have its certain mystery and complexity and you can't just reduce successful dating down to some simple steps, but we do believe you can improve your chances, and help ensure a solid foundation for a good marriage by looking to Scripture. More than any feel-good relationship expert, we've got truth on our side to help us navigate through some of the mysteries and complexities of dating.

YOU'VE GOT NOTHING TO LOSE

Dating is one of the most important processes you will ever go through, and it can potentially lead to one of the most important decisions of your life. Though this book is written from a Christian perspective, you don't have to be a Christian for our advice to work for you. It still reflects truth. Regardless of your beliefs, when you respect these steps, you will be better off. Sure, dating will always be a somewhat risky business—but doing it right is well worth the risk. We believe that *Dating 101* will help you learn to date right and find a greater depth of peace, love, and fulfillment in your own life and in your relationships. You have everything to gain, and nothing to lose.

ONE

Get a Life

It's 5:30 on a Friday afternoon, and you've got the whole weekend ahead of you. As you plop down in front of your computer to check your e-mail, your cell phone suddenly rings—it's *him*, the guy you've been seeing the last two months. Anticipating plans for a fun night out, you eagerly answer in your sweetest voice, "Hello?"

"Um, hey." He doesn't sound nearly as excited to be talking to you.

You exchange small talk about the day, and then he proceeds to tell you that he's going to play basketball with some of his guy friends tonight, and that he'll try to remember to call you tomorrow.

"What do you mean 'you'll try'?" you fire back. "Anyway, I thought we had plans for tonight!"

"Listen, I'm pretty busy these days, and . . . well, I just don't know if I have time for . . . *us*. Maybe we should think about just being friends."

"Whatever . . . I'm busy too. Have a nice time with your friends." You hang up on him, hoping you left him thinking that you couldn't care less what he does with his life or who he spends it with. But inside, your heart sinks into your stomach as you realize that this person, in whom you've invested so much time, energy, and emotion, has just put an end to something you hoped would last forever—well, at least longer than two months. You sit there, staring at your phone, thinking, *He's gonna call back any second and want to talk it out.* You keep staring at it as seconds tick by. Nothing. You feel hurt, rejected, mad, and all alone.

You spend most of the weekend on the couch, watching reruns of *That '70s Show*. By Sunday night, you don't feel any better. In fact, you are still stuck in the same emotional ditch you fell into Friday when you got the call. You replay the conversation over and over in your head and ask yourself, "What went wrong?"

Finally, a startling truth begins to emerge. You had told him you have a busy life too, but suddenly you realize that just isn't true. The truth is, you don't have a life. *This person* was your life. Your entire self-worth was wrapped up in someone else. You now see how you had put your life on hold—your education, career plans, family, interests, friends, and even your relationship with God. And now that it's over, you have nothing to sustain you—no one to call, nothing to do. Without your sweetheart, you have no life.

Okay, so maybe this illustration is a bit depressing, but believe us, we have witnessed far too many scenarios just like it. Thousands of people make bad relationship choices and end up with a lot of unnecessary pain because they ignore this first and foundational dating step: Get a life!

THE UN-LIFE

You may be thinking at this point, *But I have a life! I am busy all the time.* Are you sure? There is a huge difference between filling your life with busyness and filling your life with meaning. People who are living the un-life have one thing in common: they have put their lives on hold. They have become so consumed with finding (or keeping) someone to meet their needs and give them a sense of significance that real meaningful living has taken a backseat. They have convinced themselves that life isn't worth pursuing with any sort of passion if they don't have someone to share it with. Whether they are obsessed with finding The One or are completely jaded to the thought because their hearts have been broken, these are the ones who have contracted the fatal disease of the un-life. Here are the most common symptoms, the four Deadly Ds.

1. Desperation

A desperate person has a sense of urgency about finding someone to go out with. He is starving for someone to fill the emotional hole in his soul. Desperate people go places only to meet the opposite sex. Unfortunately, their urge-to-merge strategy inevitably hits a dead end: they end up using people, having a miserable time, developing a bad reputation, and scaring off the person they hoped to attract in the first place.

2. Dependence

Dependent people have difficulty making decisions and taking responsibility for their own lives. When a dependent person enters a relationship, he usually sucks the lifeblood out of the other person like a tick on a dog. Of course, as humans we all depend on others to some degree for certain needs. This is normal and healthy. But a person infected with the un-life will be excessively dependent on the other person to meet most of his or her needs and provide a sense of identity and significance.

3. Depression and Loneliness

Feelings of depression and loneliness are the number one complaint of people who buy into the notion that someone else can make them happy. This can take many forms, but generally it is a condition that affects the whole person: physically, emotionally, and spiritually. Most people living the un-life will experience such conditions as unhappiness, gloom, lack of energy, and withdrawal from others. It is also not uncommon to experience a significant drop in self-esteem.

The danger in depression and loneliness is that it may

begin a downward spiral. In other words, the more depressed you feel, the more likely you are to withdraw and exacerbate the situation. Eventually, this can lead to an even worse condition—clinical depression, which can involve symptoms such as loss of appetite and sleep, difficulty with concentration, problems with normal functioning, and feelings of hopelessness. This more severe form of depression calls for professional intervention such as counseling or therapy, and possibly medication. The good news is that even in the downward spiral a person can be treated and begin a reverse spiral back to having a life.

4. Detachment

Descriptions like "isolated," "withdrawn," "lonely," and "plays Xbox 24/7" describe someone who has disengaged himself from life. The desire to spend time with friends, get involved in the community, or serve at church and form other vital social relationships has vanished. It's okay to have some silence and solitude—everyone needs that now and again—but healthy, "have-a-life" people are engaged with living and forming relationships with others.

HOW TO GET A LIFE

Most of us have descended into the un-life at one time or another. The good news is that you don't need to call a doctor or go to a miracle crusade to be healed. If the four Ds describe you, then the way to a passionate, fulfilling life is through the antidote of the four Gs.

1. Get Grounded

Getting grounded is the foundation for getting a life. It is all about having a solid identity and sense of self. This includes everything from recognizing one's worth to feeling confident and secure. Individuals with a solid identity can't be shaken or devastated just because they don't have someone to date. They know who they are and don't need another human to make them feel complete.

The dominant view in our society is that human worth, value, and happiness are obtained through tangible achievement and performance. In other words, if you have money, popularity, prestige, good looks, and intelligence, *then* you have worth. The message is, "The more you have, the greater your self-esteem." This formula can literally ruin your life.

Self-worth is not something you go out and get. Self-worth is not something you buy, achieve, or obtain. It's something you *already* have. Getting grounded means embracing the fact that you are created in the image of God and have worth and value simply because you were born. Worth, based on being made in the image of God, does not fluctuate; it does not change regardless of your personality, performance, or possessions because it's based on the immutable character of God.

2. Get Grouped

Psychologists say that one of our deepest needs is to be connected with others in a meaningful way. You were created by God with the desire to be in relationships with other people, and when this God-given desire goes unmet, you will suffer. You will experience an emptiness and longing that can only be filled when you are associated with others. *Getting grouped is all about developing healthy relationships.* It is being involved with others beyond superficiality. It is about being in deeper relationships where there is trust, safety, and vulnerability.

We don't think it is a coincidence that the men and women who are passionate about life are always involved in some sort of group. It may be a service group, Bible study, or some sort of sports team, but the bottom line is that they are connected with others on a deep level. You are not an island or a Lone Ranger. You were designed to be with others!

Are you committed to a local church? Are you part of an accountability group or support group? Are you a member of a sports team? Do you participate in community service projects? Do you have people in your life who encourage you and, when necessary, graciously confront you? Do you have friends who listen to each other and can, over time, reveal their deepest concerns? If not, take this step today. Get plugged in with people in your church, college, workplace, or community, and this will help propel you out of the un-life into having a vibrant life.

3. Get Giving

Most people who are depressed, detached, or desperate usually don't even consider this next big G. Think about it—when you're feeling this way, your tendency is to focus only on your own needs and wants. In this age of self-indulgence, it seems radical to tell people to focus on someone other than themselves. *The truth is, the key to a life of misery and loneliness is seeking only to please yourself.*

Giving is about meeting the needs of others on a practical level. Do you ask, "What can I give to this relationship?" and not just, "What can I get from it?" People who are grounded and grouped are also seeking to serve and meet the needs of others. They get outside of themselves, take interest in others, and lead a rich life in the process.

4. Get Growing

In all aspects of life, things can be stagnant or growing. If you are not growing, expanding, or improving your life, you may be stagnant. You would think that almost everyone wants to be fully alive and passionate about life, but some people are little more than walking corpses because they have *stopped* growing. Growing requires the willingness to learn, improve, explore, discover, and sometimes to reach out and "boldly go where you haven't gone before."

How do you grow? It's simple. Ask yourself, "What do I have a passion for?" or "What are my skills and gifts? What am I interested in doing with my life?" For many of you, this is no problem because you are already involved in various activities that meet this requirement. However, if you are not, then plug in to some endeavor: art, drama, music, sports, volunteer work, or something else that you are interested in. Certainly, one of your most important areas for growth involves spiritual maturity—study, prayer, and church group affiliation for starters.

You may be thinking, *Wow. This sounds risky. What if I fail?* So what? Even failure is a learning, growing experience. *Success comes from good judgment, good judgment comes from experience, and experience comes from making mistakes.* The key to growing is risk.

FINDING SOMEONE ELSE WHO HAS A LIFE

So now that you know the first step of dating is to get a life, you may be thinking, *How can I meet other people who have a life?*

Great question. Unless you believe that God is going to supernaturally bring someone to your doorstep, then you must take responsibility to place yourself where there are people worth dating. Here are some ideas for expanding your playing field and finding a pool of potential dating prospects.

Church

When you meet someone at church, the chances are much greater that you will share a common spiritual bond. You already know this person either is seeking a relationship with God or has one already. Your views on morality and the sanctity of marriage will more likely be similar. Your circle of friends will also be similar. You will have a built-in support system with ministers and others who should encourage and train you in the process of building healthy relationships.

Don't fall into the trap of church hopping. Many single people are like little bees buzzing from one flower to the next, never landing in a particular church home. If you are always buzzing about, you will never stay long enough in one place to build deep friendships and you will never be a contributor to the work of God.

If you are not an active member of a local church, then get busy and find one. And don't just warm the pew, but start asking other members how you can get involved. When you are plugged in, as you will quickly discover, not only is it a great place to serve others, but it is also a target-rich environment.

Work

We don't recommend fishing off the company pier to everyone because of the obvious inherent risks of experiencing sexual harassment suits or falling in love with your boss. However, according to a recent Fortune 500 survey, the workplace is rapidly becoming a dating hot spot. Where did multibillionaire Bill Gates meet his bride? In the marketing department at Microsoft. People are working longer hours than ever before, so work has become a natural place to meet someone to date. Most companies are taking a laid-back approach to office romances.

One big advantage of meeting someone at work is the possibility that you could have a similar background. Education, socioeconomic status, and life aspirations are just a sampling of common interests you may share with a coworker. The upside of finding love at work is tremendous, but so is the downside. Let's look at some basic "9-to-5" love rules.

Rule #1: Never date someone you report to or someone who reports to you. This rule should be self-evident, but some people still don't get it.

Rule #2: Consider the outcome if your relationship doesn't work out. Would you still have to see the person all the time? Could you handle it? If an office romance goes sour, will that force you to find a new job?

Rule #3: Don't ever pursue a relationship if it is not mutual. Getting slapped with a sexual harassment suit is no laughing matter.

Friends and Family

According to surveys (our own and many others), the vast majority of successful married couples meet their partners by networking through friends and family members.

Don't be afraid to ask your friends if they know of any available guys or gals. Chances are, if your friends connect with them, then you will probably connect with them as well. Be sure to coach your friends as to what you are and are not looking for in a mate. If you don't want them involved in this process, politely tell them so.

Believe it or not, family members can be a big help here. Your family knows you better than anyone—the good, the bad, and the ugly. So when they have a poten- tial candidate for you, don't roll your eyes and brush them off too quickly. You could be missing out on a great opportunity.

Dating Services

Many moons ago, I thought dating services were only for desperate people with absolutely no social skills. I was wrong. More and more singles are bypassing the often laborious dating scene for these types of services. They offer complete confidentiality and the ability to sort through hundreds of potential dates before you ask one out. Some organizations specialize in setting you up for lunch dates only—a quick, safe way to meet dating prospects (not to mention a lot less expensive).

Before joining such an organization, check it out thoroughly. Some of them are about as trustworthy as used-car salesmen at the end of the month. Many are merely out to take advantage of your fears and prey upon your pocketbook. Others are solid organizations run with class, discretion, and professionalism.

The Internet

There's no doubt that the Internet is the fastest-growing place to meet your mate, in spite of the inherent dangers.

Since computers are all about speed, this form of connecting seems to share that same cyber-obsession for
instant love. The Internet offers hundreds of different
online venues to meet members of the opposite sex, from
dating services and chat rooms to simple personal ads
and high-dollar clubs. This is not the ideal place (the
chat-room approach being the worst), and at the very
least you run the risk of entering into a virtual relationship without the benefits of a real relationship. However,
we realize many of you use the Internet anyway. So, if
you do explore love online, be sure to obey the following
guidelines by America Online:

- Even though you may feel you've come to know
  that "special someone" through online interaction,
  DO remember that the people you meet online
  are, in fact, strangers.
- DON'T give out your phone number or address.
  Guard your personal information.
- DON'T believe everything you read. It's easy for
  someone to misguide you via online correspondence. Remember that the people at the other end
  may not be who they say they are.

- DON'T respond to correspondence that is lewd or crude or in any way makes you uncomfortable.
- If you choose to meet someone offline, use good judgment and common sense: DO meet in a public place and in a group setting.

HOW TO CREATE YOUR OWN DATING POOL

Expand Your Circle of Friends. Consider that you may have more to do with creating the circumstances for a relationship than you even realize. Many times people fail to take advantage of the opportunities that are right in front of them. It may be time to toss fate, luck, and chance out the window and begin the process of networking or placing yourself in the right environments.

The first step to expanding your circle of friends is to be willing to get out of your comfort zone. If you are not willing to try something new, then the chances are that you will remain in your rut and forgo many opportunities to expand your friendships.

The next step is to take a personal inventory. What

are your interests, hobbies, and passions in life? Select some of the interests and hobbies that you already have and take a deliberate step to meet more people who are into these same things. As you get grouped, get growing, and get giving, take a look around you. You might be pleasantly surprised to see who's standing near you!

TWO

Debunking the Dating Myths

My first meeting with Scott was rather intense. To say he was frustrated is an understatement. He began, "I'm desperate for answers. I've been searching since college and I still don't have a clue about finding someone for me. I'm tired of hearing people tell me to wait for God's timing!" Scott went on to confess, "I'm thirty-five years old and still no one in sight! Is there something wrong? Something I should be doing?" Scott had asked some legitimate questions. He was fraught with confusion and despair, and he needed some clear-cut answers.

DEMYSTIFYING THE MYTHS

Like so many other people disillusioned by the dating scene, Scott's problems stemmed from various misguided beliefs—myths—about how people end up finding a successful relationship. Just like folklore, some of these beliefs have been handed down for so long that they have started to seem true. We know many of you are walking around with a suitcase full of these dating myths and you're not even aware of it. What is worse, these faulty beliefs can actually work against you in your efforts to find a loving, lasting relationship. We hope to expose these mythical assumptions, free you from their hindrances and barriers, and discuss the corresponding truths.

Myth #1: There Is Just One Special Person for You

Wouldn't it be nice if there were someone out there designed just for you? Many people carry this hope that God, fate, or some other cosmic force has set apart someone for them. Additionally, this belief assumes that out of the six billion people on the earth, there is but one true soul mate for you. Indeed, this notion is quite appealing.

However, we believe that this kind of thinking can hurt your chances. We believe that God delights in our ability to choose and exercise responsible judgment within the context of His greater will for all mankind. Conversely, when we assume God has preselected someone for us, this can lead to a passive and irresponsible approach to mate selection. In short, it minimizes the need for common sense and it discounts the significance of human choice. When we understand that mate selection is our choice, it causes each of us to take personal responsibility for that choice once we're married. This enhances the commitment and provides a level of personal accountability. When marriage gets tough, you can't blame God or play the victim of fate. You are more inclined to say, "I trust that God led you into my life, I recognize there were good reasons why I chose you, and I take ownership of my choice."

Myth #2: If You Love God Enough, He Will Give You a Soul Mate

One of the most misinterpreted spiritual principles is taken from Psalm 37:4: "Delight yourself in the Lord and he will give you the desires of your heart." If taken the wrong way, this general principle can lead to a form of mechanical thinking about God. That is, praying hard enough, seeking His will long enough, and waiting patiently will guarantee a mate. Please understand, all these things are important and necessary but we cannot manipulate God into bringing us a partner. Some are guilty of approaching God as the big Santa Claus in the sky. If we are naughty, He punishes and withdraws His love or blessings from us. If we are nice, He will give us what we want. The goal is to balance personal responsibility with God's leading and timing.

Myth #3: There Is One, True Christian Way to Find the Love of Your Life

Within the last decade, there has been a proliferation of Christian books claiming to be the one, true way to find the love of your life. A common theme throughout is the idea that any form of modern dating is anti-Christian and unspiritual. For the sake of simplicity, we will refer to this as the "courtship model." In general, this model claims that God's way (or the biblical way) to find a mate is through a method of courtship where, through God's prompting, you identify a potential marriage partner before you ever spend intimate, one-on-one time with that person. You approach this person (and his or her parents) with your intentions to commit yourself to him or her with a view toward marriage! Does that sound a little scary?

In all seriousness, there are certainly some good principles in this model, including the emphasis on seeking God's guidance and involving the family in the process. Yet there are also many dangers, such as the tendency to overspiritualize your own selfish desires without truly examining your motives. This opens wide the door of manipulation in the name of God. Even more costly is the temptation to try to shortcut a normal, necessary process of bonding that occurs through a long-term dating relationship. The courtship model seems to place the proverbial cart before the horse by creating an expectation for commitment way too soon.

By the way, the Bible does not stipulate any particular method of mate selection. Mate selection is a social construction, not handed to us from Mt. Sinai or taught by Jesus at the Sermon on the Mount. Dating is a fine and legitimate social practice, as is courtship (potentially), and people who practice either way should seek to do so in a manner that is respectful, responsible, conscientious, and in conformity with God's moral guidelines.

Myth #4: Follow Your Heart

Ah, the ecstasy of romantic love. Nothing beats that magical experience of locking eyes with the guy or girl of your dreams across a crowded room, falling head over heels in love, and spending every waking moment with that person. If you're not yet familiar with how this thing works, you don't have to look far to see what we're talking about. In cutesy television sitcoms and weepy Hollywood movies, the prince falls in love with the princess, they get married, and everyone lives happily ever after. It all sounds great.

There's only one small problem—this is an illusion. This doesn't happen in real life. Never has. Never will. What we are saying is that *romantic love has little to do with real love.*

What is real love? This is one of the great questions of life, and for centuries philosophers have tried to define love. According to the Greeks, *eros* is the passionate form of love. It includes all the elements of that initial "feel-good" phase of a relationship: obsession, mystery, fun, excitement, and passion. *Eros* is driven by emotion. On the other hand, *agape* is the love that two people who deeply care and are concerned about each other demonstrate. *Agape* is a mature and stable kind of love—solid, enduring, and providing a sense of security.

It is best to consider romantic love and real love as two separate and distinct conditions. Real love is a decision to seek the good of another, whatever the cost. *Agape* includes nurture, support, encouragement, acceptance, and companionship. When it comes to crafting a lasting relationship, whether it be a friendship or possibly a marriage, real love far outlasts the fleeting emotions of *eros*. *Eros* is not designed to bear the weight of life's stresses. People who base their relationships only on how they *feel* rarely see such relationships last. But if you have taken the time to allow *agape* to flourish, a solid foundation of loyalty, acceptance, and trust will carry you through those tough times.

Myth #5: Don't Worry, You'll Just Know!

To be fair, there is probably a kernel of truth to this idea. At some point in the dating process, you eventually come to a place where you "just know." However, there are many important steps and guidelines that can help lead you to this point; and we believe it is crucial to have an objective basis for identifying your mate. There are specific ways to assess levels of compatibility and tools to discern whether or not you are making a wise choice.

Most people experience doubts throughout the dating process all the way to their wedding day. This hesitancy doesn't necessarily mean that the relationship is doomed. It may have nothing to do with the health or stability of the relationship. In fact, we think it is normal to experience a level of uncertainty even when you meet all the objective criteria. It is common for couples to ask us, "How can you know with 100 percent certainty if he or she is The One?" Our answer is always the same: "You *won't* know for certain until you walk back down the church aisle as husband and wife." Because ultimately, we all choose a partner based upon some measure of faith—not "blind" faith, but a decision based upon a balance of objective criteria, common sense, and subjective desire.

Myth #6: All You Need Is God

Jayne and Glen met at a wedding reception of a mutual friend and seemed to hit it off immediately. They identified their love for God and a passion for helping others.

But aside from those similarities, these two had nothing else in common! There was a fourteen-year age gap between them, a lack of chemistry for one of them, radical differences in their views on the priority of money, and significant differences of family backgrounds. When these two were challenged about their lack of compatibility in premarital counseling, they responded, "Yes, but we see eye-to-eye on the most important things (the spiritual matters) and we know God will smooth out the rough spots and cover over our differences." We firmly disagreed with this assessment.

Unfortunately, in this day and age of rampant divorce (when the divorce rate is actually higher among evangelical Christians than the secular population), spiritual compatibility is not enough to make a relationship work. You must be able to connect on a number of levels.

Myth #7: There Is Someone for Everyone

Our society puts a high premium on marriage, but for all the wrong reasons. Rather than elevating marriage because it is holy and sacred, some see it as the only real avenue for completion and wholeness. As a result, many people do not even consider "singlehood" a legitimate way of life. One of the major distortions floating' around out there is that anything less than marriage is a concession.

Let's not mince words: marriage is not for everyone, and that's okay. We believe there are several types of people who probably should be single. Consider Jesus, Paul, the pope, and Mother Teresa—we don't think they were incomplete because they were single. Who could argue that their lives were not meaningful and fulfilling simply because they were not married? Others might have a certain calling for a specific ministry. These people need support, validation, and assurance that they are not "missing out."

Because we are individuals, our sense of wholeness and completion is something we embrace within ourselves in God through Christ. It is not dependent upon someone else. In addition, it is possible to achieve intimacy without marriage or sex. David Webster, in his book *SoulCraft*, put it well when he wrote, "The longing of the soul is not for sex but for meaningful companionship." He goes on to explain that personal wholeness flows from our commitment to Christ—and nothing less will do! That's a truth you can take to the bank, and we encourage you to make this a reality in your own life, whether or not you ever get married.

THE TRUTH BEHIND THE MYTHS

These seven myths can significantly interfere with your ability to make wise choices in the dating arena. Scott was sure God would eventually bring someone to his doorstep via first class mail if he would "seek God with all his heart" and just be patient enough! He got the first part right (seek God first) but he needed permission to get off his duff!

Take a hard look at your own views toward dating. Are you waiting for God to plop someone right in front of you? Are you relying on the pitter-patter of a love-struck heart to make all your relationship decisions? Have you exalted your need to find someone over your need for God? Debunking these dating myths will put you on the path to being dateable and finding someone worth dating.

THREE

Choose Wisely

How many men and women across the globe have had their hearts and lives torn apart because they chose poorly in the dating process? Why do more than half of all marriages crater in divorce? Why do so many couples divorce each year before they have a chance to celebrate their second wedding anniversary? It's partly because men and women are simply *choosing poorly*. They're selecting the wrong people to date and then marrying one of them.

You can make a lot of bad decisions in your life and recover. You can buy the wrong car and trade it in later. You can choose the wrong college and transfer. You can take the wrong job and find another one you like better.

But if you date and then marry the wrong person, you will live with significant, negative, and lasting consequences of that decision for the rest of your life. This bears repeating: whether or not you stay married, you will live with significant, negative consequences of that decision. If you choose poorly in the dating arena, that choice can affect every area of your life.

ARE YOU MAKING POOR CHOICES?

We have identified four of the more common reasons people tend to make poor choices when it comes to dating. Each of these reasons serves to keep people from discerning the true character of those they are dating (which is, of course, the reason for dating in the first place).

Take a look at these barriers to discerning true character:

1. First-Available Syndrome
When you don't know what you are looking for and you are desperate or starved for love, you wind up compromising your standards and settling for the first available

warm body. We call this the First-Available Syndrome. Have you ever been ravenously hungry at your favorite restaurant? When the hostess asks, "Do you want smoking, non-smoking, or first available?" you respond, "*Please give me first available!*" Many people are so love-hungry that they are willing to take the first available man or woman who comes along. As radio shrink Dr. Laura Schlessinger says, "They become beggars, not choosers" in the dating process.

2. Fooled by the Externals

Nearly every week in counseling sessions or on the radio, we ask singles the all-important question: "What are you looking for in a member of the opposite sex?" By far, most people will initially say, "Well, I'm looking for a person with a good personality, someone who is outdoorsy, funny, good-looking, has a great body, money, etc." And they go on and on listing a host of superficial characteristics and personality traits.

We call this the Cotton Candy Approach. At a fair, your attention gets snagged by the cotton candy. It looks wonderful, but when you stuff a wad in your mouth, it just melts away. Oh sure, it's sweet, but you paid $5 for this huge thing that vanishes in seconds, leaving you unsatisfied. Don't get us wrong—personality and common interests are important—but alone they won't build a lasting relationship. Gazing at the externals may fool you.

3. Blinded by Sex

The Bible says, "Love covers a multitude of sins," but when it comes to dating relationships, sex covers a multitude of flaws. Sex has a way of blinding you from seeing your partner's true colors.

Sex is great in the right context (marriage), but in dating relationships, sex often clouds the relationship and shuts down communication. Men usually mistake the lovemaking for intimacy. In other words, they are duped into thinking that sex equals closeness, and therefore there is no need to work at other forms of intimacy (emotional, verbal, or spiritual). Women, on the other hand, have a tendency to confuse sex with commitment. The common misconception is that the man somehow values this relationship as unique and special. A woman will think to herself, *This must really mean love.* But some men will make love with anyone, anyway, anytime, anywhere, for just about any reason. So whether it's trading sex for love or love for sex, the sexual relationship gives one a false sense of closeness, and it blinds both parties from seeing the real person they are dating.

4. Going Too Fast

The number-one killer of people on the highway is not alcohol, it's speed. The number-one killer of potentially good relationships is also speed. When you zoom through the dating process in an attempt to bond faster than Krazy Glue, you never get to know what the person you are dating is really like. In counseling people who are in a miserable marriage or are walking around wounded from a divorce, we've heard far too many people lament, "If I had just taken the time to know this person, I would never be in this mess."

Dating is not a race to see who can get to the finish line in the shortest period of time. Dating should be a long-term process of discerning whether or not you are compatible with a person, and whether or not the two of you have what it takes to build a lasting relationship. Make this your motto: "I'd rather be single than settle."

If you desire to make wise dating choices and to know

what you want so you don't settle for the "first available," make sure that your focus is on the internals (like the Essential Character Qualities you are about to discover), save sex for marriage, and take it slow. Half the success in building a solid dating relationship that can blossom into an awesome marriage is finding the right person.

DISCERNING CHARACTER

This chapter could be summed up with one phrase: Dating is discernment. Our premise is that the dating experience is about being able to discern who this person really is. *Webster's Collegiate Dictionary* expresses this idea perfectly: Discernment is "the quality of being able to grasp and comprehend what is obscure . . . a searching that goes beyond the obvious or superficial." Think about it. That's precisely the goal of dating.

Here's why: the people you go out with are *marketing gurus.* They are always on their best behavior, always putting their best foot forward. Make no mistake, men and women will focus primarily on impressing you. Their aim is to portray themselves as charming, polite, polished, and attractive. So, you're stuck with the tremendous challenge to get beyond the mask and discover the true person underneath. Your job is to penetrate this natural tendency to impress and gain insight into who they really are. Ultimately, you're trying to discern character.

The task of discerning character is a long-term process. You can't expect to know anyone's insides without spending long periods of time with that person in many different settings and under many circumstances.

We want you to be able to look past the superficial and discern whether or not your partner has the inner goods necessary to sustain a healthy relationship. We have identified five Essential Character Qualities that you need in a mate: faithful, honest, committed, forgiving, and giving. You will find these to be extremely obvious and yet so often overlooked.

1. Faithful

A faithful person is loyal and can demonstrate an allegiance to others. As you observe this person in his social relationships or business practices, does he pass the test of loyalty? Is this someone who keeps her promises? Does this person have the capacity for fidelity? Have there been past incidences of infidelity or disloyalty in former relationships? Never continue a relationship with someone who is unfaithful unless you are willing to deal with heavy consequences.

2. Honest

An honest person is genuine and free of deception. This quality of honesty encompasses three aspects: words, actions, and personhood. First, it has to do with his word. Can you trust him to tell you the truth? Does he mean what he says? Is he prone to lies or deception (even "white" lies)? Second, honesty involves actions and behavior. Does he conduct daily behavior in an upright manner? Do others consider him to be credible, reputable, and respectable? Finally, does he have the capacity to be real, genuine, and transparent? How difficult is it to know this person? Are you able to discern his inner qualities over a period of time, or does this person have so many layers of defenses and disguises that you cannot penetrate?

3. Committed

The idea here is to find someone who can demonstrate a lifestyle of commitment, not someone who just verbalizes his commitment. Anybody can say, "Yes, I'm committed to you." But do they have what it takes to be committed to the relationship for the long haul? Dr. James Dobson speaks of two kinds of commitment: contract commitment and covenant commitment. Contract commitment is like a business agreement—if you fulfill your obligations, I'll fulfill mine. If you should violate the agreement, then I have a way out, an escape clause. This form of commitment is conditional (might as well get an attorney to draw up a marriage contract). Sadly, this seems to be the typical attitude in our society today.

On the other hand, a covenant commitment is one that emphasizes an agreement to fulfill my end of the deal, regardless of your participation. It is an unconditional agreement to hang in for life. *In fact, God has a kind of covenant relationship with all Christians. Regardless of our behavior or irresponsibility, He is committed to fulfilling His end of the agreement.* He will never leave us or forsake us, He promises eternal salvation, and He provides unconditional love and acceptance (James Dobson, Focus on the Family Radio interview, June 1998).

True love is an unconditional commitment to an imperfect person. That's the best definition of love we know of. That *is* love. However, if that sounds too ideal, too high a standard, remember the wise woman who proclaimed, "When I looked at my groom during the wedding ceremony, I suddenly realized that I couldn't honestly promise to love him perfectly. But *I could promise never to quit.*"

4. Forgiving

Forgiveness is simply releasing a person from the debt you perceive they owe you. It is about letting go of the need to punish, resent, or hold grudges when you have been wronged. When we find couples who have been happily married for thirty-five or forty years, we often ask them to sum up the secret to their success. Of course, people give many different answers, but almost always one of the reasons given is "the ability to forgive each other." If you are serious about finding someone with the character trait of forgiveness, make sure they know about the ten magic words: "I am sorry, I was wrong, will you forgive me?" If you don't know why these words possess a little bit of magic, go try them out for yourself. What kind of person are you dating? How does he resolve conflicts? Do you see an eagerness to compromise, let go, and move forward? Is there evidence of a forgiving spirit? We hope so. A successful relationship between two imperfect people must be bathed in an atmosphere of daily, mutual forgiveness.

5. Giving

This quality is not about giving material gifts but, rather, the capacity for selfless behavior. Giving means putting others first. A giver gets outside of himself and gives *to* you rather than always seeking to get *from* you. Such a person has the capacity to be "other-centered." He can demonstrate sensitivity to your needs and the ability to meet those needs. Most importantly, a giver desires to see you grow and to love you in a way that promotes wholeness. When the romantic love fades (which indeed it will), a relationship can be sustained only by a deeper kind of love, the kind that seeks to see you grow.

HELPFUL HINTS FOR DISCERNING CHARACTER

1. Crisis reveals someone's true character. When someone is faced with a difficult circumstance or crisis situation, he usually doesn't have time to think. At crucial moments, people do what comes naturally. They respond from the heart. Pay close attention to people under pressure if you want to know their true colors.

2. Character is who you are when no one is looking. If this is true, then it is vital that you place a heavy emphasis on your partner's behavior when you are together, alone, and behind closed doors. The spirit of this truth suggests that the way you are treated by your partner in private is far more important than how you are treated in public, particularly around family and friends. Many can fake character in public and some are fabulous actors when the occasion calls for it. Relatedly, if you find yourself being treated in a manner that is inappropriate or disrespectful in public (when your partner is supposed to be on "best behavior"), what does this say about this person's true character? You can bet it's even worse.

3. Friends are a window into a person's character. To really know someone, take a look at his friends. What kind of people does he hang out with? We all tend to gravitate toward those with whom we feel we have a lot in common. Furthermore, we usually become like those with whom we associate. Consider what the apostle Paul says in 1 Corinthians 15:33, "Do not be misled: 'Bad company corrupts good character.'" Rarely does the influence occur the other way around.

4. Look back on prior relationships to determine patterns of behavior. Consider whether there is a pattern of disloyalty, dishonesty, or unforgiveness in past relationships. Pay attention to how your partner talks about his or her ex-boyfriend or ex-girlfriend. Ask how your partner treated his parents while growing up and observe how he treats them now. Often this will give you clues to a person's character. In the final analysis, behavior patterns reveal more than words or promises.

5. Give it lots of time. We have continued to stress the need to give yourself a lot of time to discover who your partner truly is. It would be hard to exaggerate the importance of this truth. In fact, we've devoted a whole chapter to this matter (Chapter Five: Take It Slow).

IT'S YOUR CHOICE

Be discriminating about character. Don't compromise in this crucial area. If there is ever a time to be picky when it comes to considering your partner, this is it! All of these qualities should be *non-negotiable*. Too often we see individuals who are willing to compromise and accept three or four out of five of these qualities. These odds sound good in Las Vegas but don't hold up to the necessary requirements for a healthy marital relationship. It's okay to have your "wish list" of characteristics you want in a mate, but make sure your primary focus is on what you need—good character.

FOUR

Get Connected

In the movie *Grease*, Danny Zuko, a rebellious kid from the other side of the tracks, falls in love with Sandy, a beautiful blue-eyed blond with a squeaky clean image. The only thing Danny and Sandy have in common is their sizzling hot attraction to one another, yet they fall in love and make a few compromises: she puts on a black leather jacket, and he joins the track team. At the end-of-school carnival, the entire cast breaks out dancing, singing, and generally has a good ol' time while the unlikely duo drives off into the sunset.

The "opposites attract" relationship works great on the big screen, but in reality it's extremely difficult to pull off. Tragically, many people actually seek out this kind of pairing under the illusion that it is a good way to form an enduring bond! While it is true that opposites do attract sometimes, this attraction usually doesn't hold up to the difficulties of real life and commitment. The truth is that the most healthy relationships are ones in which there are a lot of similarities between partners, where the similarities far outweigh the differences.

In counseling a multitude of couples, we have discovered that there are certain types of relationships that are more likely to last and be healthy. We call these Equally Yoked Relationships. This chapter will show you what to look for in order to establish an Equally Yoked Relationship.

EQUALLY YOKED RELATIONSHIPS

In the Bible, there is a passage that exhorts Christians not to be yoked with non-Christians. A yoke was a strong wooden bar placed around the necks of oxen and then connected to a plow. The trick was to yoke together two oxen of equal strength so they would plow a field in a straight line. Unequally yoked oxen would simply move around in circles. The Bible uses this metaphor to warn of the dangers of believers being "yoked" together with unbelievers—two people who are ultimately headed in opposite directions. A relationship, by definition, is the connecting of persons. Equally Yoked Relationships connect on three general levels: *spiritual*, *physical*, and *social*.

1. The Spiritual Connection

If you cannot connect with your partner on a spiritual level, your relationship is headed for disaster. What you believe about God, how you pray, where you worship, which holidays you celebrate, and which books you hold to be sacred are just a few components that make up your spiritual belief system. Your spirituality and how that is expressed is the most intense and intimate part of you.

From a Christian perspective, you should date only Christians. There is no exception. Everyone thinks, "But my relationship is different." Trust us, it is not. If you could just listen to the tales of relational carnage that we hear from married couples trying to keep it together as they vehemently oppose each other on an issue that stems from their deeply held religious convictions, you would flee such a dating relationship. On your side of the altar you simply can't know how incredibly contentious it gets on the other side.

Many Christians fall into the trap of dating a non-Christian because they never bother asking that person about his or her beliefs. Others simply assume that the person they are dating is a Christian because after all, "He told me he was a Christian." Only God knows who is a real Christian and who is not, but He does lay down a few guidelines to help you discern if the person you are going out with is a genuine Christian.

Personal testimony. Someone who knows Jesus Christ will be able to point to a certain time in life when he or she personally trusted Him as Lord and Savior. A Christian makes a conscious decision to repent of sin and to trust and follow Christ. A believer feels no fear or shame acknowledging and discussing this critical life foundation.

Changed lifestyle. A Christian seeks to live according to the principles set forth in the Bible. Believers attend church and desire to hang out with other Christians. They seek to love others and bring them into a personal relationship with Christ. Christians value sexual purity and don't take advantage of their partners. They desire to study, pray, and apply the Scriptures to their lives. They forgive others because they have received abundant forgiveness from God.

Be sure that you are dating a person with whom you can connect on a spiritual level. If you are a Christian, be certain that your partner has had a "real deal" encounter with Christ and, as a result, has a changed life. Tremendous joy and intimacy will flow within the couple who connects on the spiritual level. On the other hand, tremendous heartache and frustration will occur when two people are unable to connect and share this most intimate part of their lives.

2. The Physical Connection

Not only must you connect on the spiritual level, but you also must connect with your partner on the physical level. While this may seem obvious, we are asked with astounding frequency about the importance of this dimension. *Being sexually attracted to your partner is a prerequisite for a healthy relationship.* Having a spiritual connection is not enough. You must have that spark, that chemistry, that attraction that draws you to that person like a magnet.

Most people overdose on the hormonal attraction thing and forget about the other crucial levels of connections, but still we meet people who hang on to others without any romantic attraction. There are no "Ten Steps to Developing Chemistry." All great relationships have some element of chemistry, and you either have it or you don't. Most likely you will never grow into it or somehow make it happen.

3. The Social Connection

Some people often ignore or neglect social compatibility, though this very area creates lots of stresses on relationships. Social compatibility primarily concerns family patterns and social relating, and we'll consider them in order.

Family matters. The old saying "the apple doesn't fall far from the tree" usually holds true. Many of your perspectives (big and small) on life stem directly from your family upbringing. If you grew up in a home in which you received love, support, encouragement, and security from your parents, then you probably have a good foundation for building a relationship with another person. If not, you will have to work a little harder to develop such a relationship.

Not too long ago, society was less mobile; people married their next-door neighbors, or at least someone from their hometown. One easily found someone who shared similar family and cultural perspectives. However, with today's overwhelming divorce rate, blended families, and frequent transcontinental moves, the difficulty in finding a partner with a similar family background skyrockets. Nonetheless, this remains a tremendously vital area for seeking compatibility because of the many related issues.

Some of the more important issues associated with family background include: holiday customs, expectations about spousal roles, finances, rearing children, in-laws, work ethic, and resolving conflict. Given the pervasive influence of one's family life, it remains important that you seek to connect on this level.

Social relating. The other area of connecting at the social level deals with patterns of relating. This dimension of a relationship covers a wide variety of concerns, including level of social involvement, gravitation toward similar types of people, communication style, and intellectual compatibility/educational background.

What does it mean to be equally yoked? Well, similarities between people make life together much simpler.

Partnerships, by necessity, involve compromise, and people can reach these compromises more easily when they share common values and interests. This holds true whether you're going on a date and picking a movie or whether you're married and deciding where to rear your children. By contrast, being unequally yoked to someone with whom you have few affinities can turn even the smallest of decisions into big problems. Sure, sometimes opposites can attract, but for a stable relationship, get connected with someone similar.

FIVE

Take It Slow

Remember when you were a kid and you could hardly wait 'til Christmas? No matter how many times your Sunday school teacher said, "Jesus is the reason for the season," Christmas meant one thing to you then: presents. You would scour the house, hoping to catch a glimpse of what might be awaiting you Christmas morning. Or maybe you were one of those who shook every present under the tree. When it comes to Christmas, every kid feels the same: "It just can't get here fast enough."

Ever wonder why relationships with the opposite sex feel the same way? Once love is in the air, things just can't move fast enough. You feel as though you need to see this person every waking moment, or at least be on the phone with him or her. He or she is all you think about, all you dream about, all you talk about. If you aren't together, you're miserable, and you make everyone around you miserable too.

What is it about relationships that compels us to rush things—rush to go out again, rush to hold hands, rush to have that first kiss? We're convinced that the number one reason couples divorce is not money, sex, or infidelity, but rather because the decision to get married was made too quickly.

If you have ever listened to my (Ben's) *Single Connection* radio program or attended one of our relationship seminars, you know the most important dating principle. It's really an essential commandment: *"Take it slow, get to know."* Take it slow and get to know the person before you buy the ring or practice how his last name sounds with your first name. *No one enters a marriage with the goal of getting a divorce, but still millions divorce.* Why? They didn't take the time to get to know the person with whom they were going to spend the rest of their life.

THREE REASONS TO TAKE IT SLOW

Most couples don't take nearly enough time to get to know the person they are about to marry. But there is a direct correlation between length of courtship and marital satisfaction. With marriages crashing and burning all over the place, don't you want to do everything possible to make yours last?

1. You do not get to know a person in a short period of time.

When you marry someone, you want to know what that person is really like before you make that lifelong commitment to love for better or worse, richer or poorer, in sickness and in health, 'til death do you part.

If you think you can really get to know a person's true colors in a three-to-six month dating period, then you are either psychic or psycho. Believe me, when it comes to fervent explanations as to why your relationship is different, I've heard it all. For example, (1) you know God has told you this is the one you are to marry, or (2) you have never felt this way about anyone else, or (3) you have stayed up all night talking, and you know everything there is to know about each other. Yada, yada, yada. Trust me, you still need to take it slow. It's impossible to really get to know someone in such a short period of time.

Too many people jump into marriages after a brief courtship, only to discover their mates are abusive, chronic debtors, or workaholics. It's pretty easy to fake it in a three- to six-month period. Almost anyone can put on a good act for a few months. Plus, if you throw in the most effective device for both covering a person's true character and destroying discernment—*sex*—then you have a formula for disaster. The safest way to make a lasting relationship is by investing time to get to know that person.

2. You need time to go through the necessary stages of bonding.

Most relationships can be broken down into four stages of bonding and attachment. The first stage is the *Scouting Stage*, which is when you are simply testing the waters to see if you like this person or not. The second stage is what we call the *Infatuation Stage*, in which you are madly in love with this person, and absolutely blind to his or her faults. Some also call this the *Honeymoon Phase* of a relationship, which lasts anywhere from three to nine months, depending how good both parties are at faking it. The third phase is the *Reality Bites Stage*, which occurs when you wake up and realize this "perfect person" has some glaring chinks in the armor. The fourth stage is the *Fish or Cut Bait Stage*. This stage is the one where you decide if you should marry this person or let go. Each stage needs its time in order for you to really bond.

3. You protect yourself from getting attached too quickly.

Another reason you should take it slow is that you guard yourself from getting emotionally attached to too many people. When you have an initial attraction to someone that is so strong you can feel your heart beating through your chest, it's difficult not to react to that powerful feeling. I know lots of single men and women who are romantic love junkies. They live for that indescribable, magical spark that happens when two people feel that instant sense of closeness. Spending eight hours together on the first date, allowing things to progress too quickly in the physical area, and seeing each other every single day is a formula for short-term pleasure, long-term pain.

Of course, one day they wake up and realize they are absolutely sick of being with this person, because they smothered each other so much that the love flame was extinguished. Others have a worse fate: they never slow down long enough to catch a breath, and the next thing you know they find themselves dressed in a tuxedo or a white dress about to pledge their lives to someone they have known for a whopping four months.

If you take it slow early on, you won't become a love junkie or marry someone you barely know. When you seek to take it slow, you hold off any physical affection until you are ready to enter an exclusive dating relationship. This protects you from giving your heart and body to someone you don't really know and allows you to get out of a relationship without having invested too much emotional and spiritual energy on the wrong person.

SEVEN SLOW-MOTION DATING STRATEGIES

Because of the natural tendency to speed at the beginning of a relationship, you must have a strategy locked in place to help you keep it in low gear. Here is our list of seven strategies that must be employed:

1. Make the Two-Year Commitment

Nothing will help you take it slow more than deciding before you get involved that, no matter how great it feels, you are going to invest two years in getting to know this person before you commit to marriage. This does not mean you enter a long, drawn-out relationship with every person that you meet. It simply means that when you believe you have found the right person, you allow for at least two years from your first date to your wedding date.

The two-year commitment often freaks out singles and single-again people who feel like they are going to explode if their urge to merge is not satisfied soon. However, just think of this commitment as a long-term investment that will pay handsome dividends into your emotional, spiritual, and relational bank. What is a short two years in a thirty-year marriage?

2. Make Your First Date Short and Casual

When you start off slow, it's a whole lot easier to continue that process. Go out to lunch with someone on a first date, or give yourself a curfew if the date is in the evening, and stick to it.

Another way to keep it slow in the beginning is to limit the number of times you see a person in a week. This will serve two purposes. First, it will force you to take it slow so that you don't attempt to bond too quickly. Second, you will probably become more attractive to the person you are seeing because you will not appear to be overly dependent on a relationship to make you happy. The other person will be able to tell that you have a life.

3. Don't Volunteer Too Much Information Up Front

Too many eager daters spill their guts to a potential partner on the very first date. Don't take the, "Hi, my name is Chris, let me tell you my darkest childhood memory and why I hate my father" approach with someone you don't even know. When you share too much too soon, it's as if you are verbally vomiting on that person.

Many singles justify their proclivity to do this by saying, "I'm sick and tired of playing games. I want to be real." Listen, there is a time to be open and vulnerable, but it's not when you are just getting to know someone. Practice patience and prudence. There is another term for people who volunteer too much information up front: drunk.

4. Delay Physical Affection

Holding hands, hugging, and kissing should be symbols of a secure relationship, not a means of *gaining* a secure relationship. When you bring touch into your relationship, the stakes increase, and it makes ending the relationship all the more difficult. The Icing on the Cake Theory says that affection should be the finishing touches of a secure friendship that is budding into a committed dating relationship. In a day when most men expect to have sex after the third date this may sound archaic, but it's the only way to develop healthy dating patterns.

Women especially need to take a firm stand here and not cave in to a man's advances. Far too many women have had the audacity to say to me, "Well, if I don't have sex with him, he'll leave." Fine—let him leave! *If you allow a man to have his way with you, you will never, ever be respected by him.*

5. Stay Connected with Your Friends

One of the worst things you can do in the dating process

is to ditch your friends the moment you feel like you've met someone special. Maintaining your gender-specific friendships will prevent you from getting sucked into the relational speed zone. When some people fall in love, they have a tendency to punt their friends and OD on their new romantic interest. This kind of behavior usually hacks off their friends and scares off the potential romance. Stay connected with your friends. You may need them on the flip side, not to mention the fact that you will definitely need their advice and feedback throughout the dating process.

6. Do Not Pray Together

The "let's be prayer partners" approach sounds sweet and spiritual on the surface, but can actually be used as a form of manipulation. Praying is one of the most intimate experiences you can ever have. Consider the fact that when you pray with someone you hardly know, you are encouraging a bond that can be more intense than even physical affection or sex. There is a fine line between spirituality and sexuality, and people who do not respect that line are in danger of getting burned. There will be plenty of time down the road to pray together.

7. Don't Mention the "M" Word

If you really want to create emotional chaos and unrealistic expectations in the early stages of a dating relationship, then just mention the "M" word. *Marriage.* Once you throw out the "M" word, you can't take it back. It changes the entire relationship and puts undue pressure on the two of you. Men sometimes manipulate women by making a passing remark like, "Maybe some day we will get married," and women often fall for the line as if it were an inevitable truth. Women, on the other hand, sometimes scare off potential partners by talking about marriage before the relationship has had a chance to mature. The bottom line is, keep your mouth shut. No matter how many little coincidences have occurred that prove you are destined to be united and in spite of hints dropped by overeager parents and well-meaning friends, resist. Wait. Don't talk about marriage until the timing is right.

Take it slow. Avoid the heartache of emotionally or physically bonding with someone too early and scattering yourself. You'll be glad you enjoyed the journey of watching your relationship develop gradually.

SIX

Walk Away . . .
from the Wrong One

Aren't you amazed at the dangerous and downright idiotic things we will tolerate in another person when we make the false assumption that he or she is worth dating?

Whitney called my radio show to tell me how she was madly in love with Tom. Everything about their relationship was wonderful, except for one minor problem—he was married. After I gave her a compassionate verbal lashing, my next caller, Diedra, picked up where I left off and continued to chastise Whitney. I had a cow when Diedra later confessed to me that she had been living with a man for five years, and he was currently cheating on her. Talk about the need to remove a two-by-four from your own eye before removing a splinter from another's. Yikes!

Now those are extreme situations, but most of us would confess (I know I do) that we have hung on to people in a dating relationship far too long, when we knew for months that it was not going to work out. One of the important steps in the process of dating is learning how to eliminate those who are not good candidates for a long-term relationship. If you can discern who is *not* worth dating, then you are well on your way to finding someone who is. This chapter will give you eight ways to know if someone is not The One and five tips on how to break it off, should you face this unfortunate dilemma. Since you can never underestimate the power of denial, let's first take a look at some reasons (or better yet, rationalizations) as to why you may be dating Mr. or Ms. Wrong.

EIGHT REASONS YOU'RE DATING THE WRONG ONE

1. *"I know I can fix this one."* If you feel the need to renovate the one you're with or reason that marriage will

change the one you love, think again. Marry a person, not a project.

2. *"But I love him."* If you believe that love can conquer all, including huge credit card debt, weak character, and a depressive personality, you are mistaken. True love allows others to experience the negative consequences of their choices and does not always cover for them.

3. *"It's better than being alone."* On some level, this line of reasoning is understandable. Yet when a relationship is damaging to your growth or sense of self, the cost is much greater than the short-term benefit.

4. *"I've invested too much time and energy."* When you have poured your heart and soul into another person, it is extremely difficult to let go. I do empathize with this rationalization, but know from experience that you don't want to forge ahead when you see major red flags.

5. *"I'm scared of what the person might do if . . ."* If you are anxious that he or she might do something crazy if you break up, then just think a little bit about what you are saying. The fact that you have these kinds of concerns about this individual should make you scared about your own lack of judgment.

6. "I'm afraid I will hurt him/her." Ending a relationship is usually difficult, touchy, and painful for both parties. Sometimes healthy decisions and responsible action are painful.

7. "I need the financial security this relationship offers me." The Beatles were right; money can't buy you love. But it sure can buy you the illusion of security. If you continue to hang on for this reason, you will be headed for a passionless, empty marriage.

8. "God's called me to carry this cross." Do you really believe that God wants you to date or marry someone who is unhealthy for you? Sometimes God does take us down a rough road, but let's not be presumptuous or foolish and assume He wants you to make a poor choice in the dating arena.

I know it is tempting to close your eyes, rationalize, and pray that things will change, but more than likely they will not. You know you are "hanging on" when you are always trying to justify your relationship or dreaming about the person you hope he or she will become. If you are stubborn or not convinced yet, then read on. Here are eight good reasons this is definitely not the person for you.

EIGHT REASONS TO WALK AWAY

1. You are not in sync spiritually. So many people are so eager to fall in love or find The One that they ignore their spiritual compatibility all together, until they wake up one morning and realize how their entire relationship has been infected by this void. If you are not in sync spiritually, you cannot connect with this person heart to heart.

2. You see major character flaws. After listening to Darren go on and on about all the bizarre personal traits he was tolerating in his relationship with Bianca, I finally stopped him and said, "She must be incredibly good-looking." Darren was surprised and responded, "Why would you say that?" I went on to tell him that there was no other way anyone would put up with the major character flaws he mentioned, unless he was blinded by looks or sex. If someone is dishonest, mean, angry, emotionally unstable, or unfaithful, this is a sign. Don't wait for a voice from on high to move on.

3. You are not romantically attracted. If you are not attracted to the person you are dating, something is wrong. Don't forge ahead, hoping that things will change. Things *will* change; you will find someone else to whom you *are* attracted and wonder why you settled for second best. I've seen many a "spiritual" man or woman hang on to a potential marriage partner for years, praying that God would zap them with the ability to be attracted to their partner. I've talked to women whose marriages ended in divorce because they were attracted to his "love for God," but turned off in every other way. If you think romantic attraction is unimportant to God, I challenge you to read Song of Solomon.

4. *You are having to work too hard.* It is often stated that any good relationship requires hard work and continual maintenance, but if you are constantly striving during the dating stage to have fun and to experience a sense of unity, then your marriage will be a living Alcatraz. The daily miscommunication and evaluation will rob you of the necessary joy and laughter that any good soul-mate relationship should have.

5. *You are constantly fighting.* If you are in a relationship that is characterized more by your quarrels than your intimate conversations, then you are headed for trouble. There needs to be healthy conflict in any

relationship or you cannot grow, but if your relationship is one big battleground, that is a sign of incompatibility.

6. *You have been abused.* If you have been physically or verbally abused by your dating partner, get out and move on—no questions asked. We have zero tolerance for men who would strike, push, or verbally abuse their girlfriends (and you should too). I don't care how many times he said, "I'm sorry; it will never happen again." Don't give him a second chance. You do not want to be a feature story of domestic violence on the evening news.

7. *You are not top priority in his or her life.* Ashlyn always felt she was low on the totem pole of Terry's priorities. She was right. He never did anything special for her on Valentine's Day or her birthday. He would go out with the guys on the weekends and squeeze time in with Ashlyn when it was convenient for him. She allowed this to continue until the day she got up enough nerve to call it off. Terry was stunned and pleaded to get back together, but she was tired of being treated like leftovers. Catch a clue from Ashlyn. If you are not a priority in his or her life today, you never will be.

8. You are constantly changing to please him or her. A chameleon is a tiny lizard whose skin changes into the color of its environment. When you are trying to change your personality, friends, hair color, or taste in movies just to please the person you are going out with, then you are a chameleon dater. You want someone to be attracted to you for who you are, not the phony skin you are wearing to blend in and make the other person feel good. One day, your true colors will show.

The greatest temptation is to blow off some or all of the eight good reasons you just read. Take a look at some of the more common justifications: "It's so hard to find someone out there who has it together," or "Once we get married, he or she will start going to church, being more romantic, stop drinking with friends, cheating on me. . ."

Listen, please. Marriage will not change this person. Marriage will magnify your problems, not cure them. Sure, it will be painful to walk away, but it will be much more painful to get a divorce or attempt to endure an unhealthy, stagnant marriage. If you know this person isn't right for you, but you aren't sure about how to end it, then follow these guidelines.

HOW DO YOU BREAK IT OFF?

Many people who find themselves in an unhealthy relationship attempt the avoiding or passive-aggressive approach (they simply do nothing). Instead of seeking closure, they just stop calling, start refusing to go out, and try to let the relationship die without any confrontation. If you know that the relationship is over in your heart and mind, then be respectful and take action. Here are some helpful guidelines on how to break up.

1. Immediately. Do not waste any more of your time or your partner's time by prolonging the inevitable. You have to work through the fact that feelings will get hurt, not everyone is going to be happy, and life in general can be painful. If you play games and hold on, all you are doing is enlarging the emotional wound. Sure, you are a month away from your one-year anniversary or it's too close to Christmas or it's the day after Groundhog Day or your partner just got laid off. It is never a good time to break up. But now is always better than later. That's why you must act immediately!

2. Honestly. Be open, honest, direct, and sincere. Get to the point and don't linger in the realm of ambiguity.

Make sure you do so in the spirit of letting your yes be yes and your no be no.

3. Tactfully. This is not your time to get even for every cruel thing that has been done to you. Nor is it appropriate to get into the specific and gory details, or it will turn into a "let's see if we can work this thing out" session. Be honest but tactful. Do not read off a list of every reason as to why he or she is not right for you. If you are emotional, take a deep breath and try to calm down. You may want to write out what you are going to say and read it to the person. Be challenged by Ephesians 4:29: "Let no unwholesome word proceed out of your mouth, but only what is edifying for the need of the moment. Remember to exhibit compassion and grace." (our paraphrase)

4. Courageously. You can do it. Breaking up is one of the most difficult things in the world to do. You may love this person on some level; there have been some good times shared, and he or she may be a wonderful person in many ways, but don't lose sight of the fact that you are not a match. You are doing the other person a favor as well as yourself. Be strong and courageous. It may be one of the best decisions you ever make.

5. Completely. This is where a person hesitates to make

a clean break. You say it's over, but you call the next week to see how he or she is doing. Or you send an e-mail or call a month from now when you are feeling lonely. Don't play games with someone's heart. If you still have some form of ongoing communication with your ex, then you are not officially broken up yet. This post-relationship syndrome is common with daters who do not want to burn their bridges. You can't be "good friends" with your ex; you have gone too far to go back to a superficial kind of friendship. When you call it off, be sure it is a clean break. No follow-up phone calls, e-mails, letters, or casual cups of coffee to "just see how he or she is doing."

When it's time to end it, don't delay. Do it immediately, honestly, tactfully, courageously, and completely.

SEVEN

Make It Work . . . with the Right One

Okay, so what do you do after you've dated someone for awhile and you begin thinking they are The One for you? You've considered all the major issues and you've confirmed a natural fit: you have strong relational compatibility and good character, and you connect spiritually. You have been wise, discriminating, cautious, and prayerful. Congratulations! But now what? Do you wait a little longer just in case? Do you jump in to marriage feet first? We want to help you take it to that ultimate place—marital success.

This chapter has a twofold purpose. First, we will offer suggestions on how to manage that delicate time from *exclusivity* through *engagement.* Second, we will offer realistic guidelines to help you enter marriage with a foundation of strength. Once you believe you have found The One, this phase of your relationship is crucial, as you are already building a foundation for your future marriage.

Let's take a look at some of the don'ts and do's of building a great foundation for keeping The Right One.

THE DON'TS OF KEEPING THE ONE

1. Don't wait for a sign from heaven.

If you have dated exclusively for two or more years, you're out of college, and you know that you connect in the ways we've outlined in this book, there is no need to drag out the inevitable. In fact, you may be doing more harm than good. At some point your faith and caution begin to look like doubt and fear. You could be communicating the wrong message by playing it too safe and therefore planting seeds of insecurity. Most often it is the man who prolongs by offering one rationalization and excuse after another in order to buy time. This approach can actually be a cover for a lack of faith, confidence, or security.

2. Don't pressure your partner if you are within the two-year time frame.

It is not unusual for one person to be more certain about the relationship than the other. Assuming you are some-where within the first six and twenty-four months of the relationship, you may have a strong conviction that he or she is The One much sooner than your partner. The worst thing you can do is try to manipulate the other person's feelings or challenge his or her thinking too soon. You should give your partner the freedom to evaluate the relationship on his or her own time (within reason).

3. Don't isolate yourselves.

Whenever we encounter couples who isolate themselves and keep their relationship ultra-private, it usually signi-fies a level of immaturity or it indicates a possible warning sign. Some are tempted to ignore their friends and hide in seclusion with their beloved. After all, the thinking goes, I've found my soul mate and he or she is all I need. When you think you have found The One, don't exclude others from your lives together. When you surround your rela-tionship with supportive friends and family, you give them the opportunity to support and encourage you toward building a lasting marriage.

4. Don't experiment with living together.

In this day and age of moral relativity, the predominant (conventional) wisdom encourages couples to test their compatibility by living together. Ironically, according to a study by the National Marriage Project at Rutgers University (September 1999), "living together is not marriage friendly." This study states that couples who live together before marriage are forty-eight percent more likely to divorce than those who don't. Among the findings was that people who cohabit report lower levels of happiness and much greater chances of domestic violence. Don't be a statistic; save living together for marriage.

A BETTER WAY TO CLOSE THE DEAL

When you and your partner have a reasonable sense that you are meant to be together, besides avoiding the don'ts, we would like to offer four critical guidelines (the do's) to help you prepare for a successful lifetime union.

1. Appoint an Advisory Board

One of the most important things you can do to enhance your odds of success is to surround yourself with a group of people who can support you and offer priceless feedback—we call this an advisory board. Fifty years ago, this concept of including community was natural and automatic. Back then, it seems everybody was involved in the love life of a given couple. Family members, neighbors, pastors—all had a hand in bringing people together, keeping them accountable, and encouraging their growth toward marriage. Now, it may go against your natural inclination, but you need to surround yourself with people who will assist you in the process of uniting as one. Making your relationship a part of the larger community has to be an intentional process. This is what we mean by appointing an advisory board. Have your closest, trusted friends and family members aid in this important decision. We would suggest that each of you seek out those people who know you best and who are not afraid to tell you the truth. Make sure you appoint people who interact with you regularly as a couple. That way, they have a firsthand account of the relationship in context. As such, they can offer objective perspectives based upon what they observe, not from secondhand information you have told them about the relationship.

We hope it is already understood that God Himself is to take the position of Chairman of the board. We assume you will be prayerful and sensitive to God's true leading as you submit to His authority and continue toward the path of engagement and ultimately marriage. To help you discern God's leading, we would suggest that you pick up a copy of Gary Friesen's book *Decision Making and the Will of God*.

2. Define the Relationship Sooner than Later

When you have been in an ongoing relationship for a period of one year or more (assuming you are at least twenty-two years of age), it is certainly legitimate to begin the process of defining the relationship. As we have stated, this is not a time to pressure your partner for a commitment to marriage, but it is a time to be open, honest, and direct about your expectations for a future together. Obviously, the longer you've been in the dating scene and the older you are, the more proficient you become at eliminating those who are not The One.

Remember, if you have found someone with all the potential to be The One, until you have been dating for at least a year, you have no basis for real love. Prior to one year, you may be infatuated or "in lust." But make no mistake, real love takes time. Once you decide to define the relationship, you must seek to clarify your thoughts, feelings, and intentions regarding the future of the relationship.

Some of the most prevalent relationship killers are the hidden expectations and unspoken assumptions in many otherwise promising relationships. Too often people will stay in a holding pattern or let the more passive partner dictate the length of the dating. Unfortunately, this is not out of respect as much as it is out of fear. Don't be afraid to gently confront your partner about lack of communication, clarity, or follow-through if this describes him or her. The luxury of having free-choice mate selection (as opposed to arrangement) is the length of time you have to get to know each other and make wise choices based upon discernment. However, some take this luxury too far and spend seven years "getting to know" their partner. This is taking a good thing too far. Eventually, this can become counterproductive and you may reach a point of no return.

3. Seek Relationship Counseling (ASAP)

Once you and your partner believe each other to be The One, then it becomes critical that you seek out pre-engagement or premarital counseling as soon as possible. If I had a nickel for every couple that called me for "counseling" after their wedding invitations were already sent out, I'd be hobnobbing with Donald Trump. Quite frankly, it verges on presumption and arrogance to think that a couple can casually waltz into premarital counseling five weeks before their wedding and expect to achieve significant results. The whole point of counseling is to confirm, clarify, and objectively sort out the wisdom of this monumental decision. It is also a time to identify strengths and weaknesses of the relationship as well as identify the issues that each partner will bring to the relationship. Granted, one of the greatest concerns that couples encounter is the fear that counseling will pick apart and destroy their relationship. Keep in mind that a counselor is not the bad guy wanting to interrogate or tear you down, but is there to support you and help you.

4. Nurture the Relationship

A committed relationship is no haven for the lazy. It's certainly not a place where you can sit around like a queen or king and never lift a finger. A relationship takes work, and it is only as good as what you are willing to invest. As much as a plant needs sun, soil, and water to live and grow, so too a relationship needs even more nurturing. Now is the time to nurture the relationship. Get actively engaged in the process of helping your partner grow and become a better person. Seek to develop and mature your relationship. Don't be content to ride on the coattails of infatuation and romantic love—get busy establishing and building that soul-and-spirit connection.

Once you have discovered you are spiritually compatible, you need to work on developing and growing that aspect of your relationship together. Buy books or devotionals, go to relationship conferences, and seek married mentors in order to grow relationally and spiritually together. One of the best premarital books available is *Saving Your Marriage Before It Starts* by Drs. Les and Leslie Parrott. For those who want to plunge into the theological and philosophical depths of marriage, take a look at *The Mystery of Marriage* by Mike Mason.

REMEMBER THE SOURCE OF LOVE

Our final words of advice for making your relationship work is *remember the source of your love.* As a newlywed in the first few years of marriage, I (Sam) recall feeling overwhelmed with all the requirements of a sacrificial love in marriage. It was exhausting to consider all the things I am required to do as a Christian husband. These expectations are extraordinary and impossible to fulfill. For starters, I'm commanded to love my wife as Christ loves the church and to lay down my life for her (oh, that's an easy one!). I'm called to make sacrifices for her; to put her needs above mine. In addition, I'm supposed to accept, affirm, appreciate, challenge, comfort, encourage, forgive, inspire, lead, respect, support, and validate her. And to top it all off, she wants me to share my feelings from time to time!

It was a relief to discover, several years later, that I wasn't supposed to be able to love anyone like that. God has no expectations for me to love this way on my own. He must do these things through me. When my relationship with God is stable, these loving qualities flow through me. When I am spiritually distant and attempting to live life on my own or according to my own agenda, I fail miserably in my attempts. Therefore I must keep my focus predominantly on staying connected, tapped into the Source of love. In the gospel of John, Jesus said, "I am the vine; you are the branches. If a man remains in me and I in him, he will bear much fruit; apart from me you can do nothing" (15:5).

Christ used the vine and branch illustration to represent our need to stay connected to Him daily, hourly, even minute by minute. Christ identified Himself as the "true vine" (John 15:1), and we (as Christians) are the branches. The vine gives life and sustenance to the branch and allows it to grow and bear fruit. It's no exaggeration to say that we are often inadequate, insufficient, and utterly dependent upon Christ to live His life through us every day. Only through Christ can we bear the fruit of the Spirit.

Do you want to love as Christ loves us? Want to be able to serve, forgive, and inspire your partner? Want to have joy, peace, or patience? Then make it your goal to stay connected to "the vine," that is, Christ. Only He, the Source and Perfector of your love, can cause you to bear fruit that will give you an amazing, long-lasting marriage.

CONCLUSION

We hope that by now you feel equipped with some clear steps that will enable you to survive and thrive in the world of dating. When your approach to dating is passive, reactive, haphazard, or superstitious, you will always come up short. But when you choose to take responsibility and commit to balance God's leading and direction with a plan of action, you will be well on your way to finding a relationship that will work. Don't compromise or settle for less. Get a life. Get over the dating myths. Make wise choices. Get equally yoked. Take it slow. Walk away from the wrong ones. Make it work with the right one. And—above all—enjoy the process along the way!

About the Authors

BEN YOUNG, M.Div., leads seminars on how to build successful dating and marriage relationships. He is a teaching pastor at the 40,000-member Second Baptist Church in Houston, Texas.

SAMUEL ADAMS, Psy.D., is a licensed psychologist. He earned his master's from Western Seminary and a doctorate from George Fox University. He maintains a full-time counseling practice in Austin, Texas.